Annapolis

CORNERSTONES OF FREEDOM
SECOND SERIES

R. Conrad Stein

Children's Press®
A Division of Scholastic Inc.
New York • Toronto • London • Auckland • Sydney
Mexico City • New Delhi • Hong Kong
Danbury, Connecticut

Photographs ©2004: Brown Brothers: 4, 16, 18, 19, 22; Corbis Images: 6 (Bettmann), 35 left (Duomo), 7, 44 top left (Kevin Fleming), 31 (Annie Griffiths), 24 (Robert Maass), 25, 45 bottom (Douglas Peebles), 40 (Lee Snider), 17 (Peter Turnley); Getty Images: 34, 35 right; Hulton|Archive/Getty Images: 21; North Wind Picture Archives: 11; Roger Miller: cover bottom, cover top, 8, 9, 27, 29, 30, 32, 33, 37, 38, 39, 41, 45 center, 45 top; Superstock, Inc./Jack Novak: 23; U.S. Naval Academy Archives: 3, 44 bottom (Shannon Bosserman), 28 (Wayne McCrea), 10,13, 15, 36, 44 top right; U.S. Naval Historical Center: 12, 14, 20.

Library of Congress Cataloging-in-Publication Data
Stein, R. Conrad.
  Annapolis / R. Conrad Stein.
      p. cm. — (Cornerstones of freedom. Second series)
Summary: Discusses the history of the United States Naval Academy at Annapolis, Maryland, its distinguished graduates, and student life.
Includes bibliographical references and index.
   ISBN 0-516-24229-6
   1. United States Naval Academy—Juvenile literature. [1. United States Naval Academy—History.] I. Title. II. Series.
V415.L1.S734 2003
359'.0071'173—dc21

                                       2003009094

1 2 3 4 5 6 7 8 9 10 R 13 12 11 10 09 08 07 06 05 04

W

E COME FROM ALL PARTS OF THIS NATION

WE ENTER THESE GATES TO LEARN

WE GO FORTH TO SERVE

—From a **placard** *near the main gate of the U.S. Naval Academy at Annapolis, Maryland. The placard was presented to the Academy by the graduating class of 1946.*

★ ★ ★ ★

A DISTINGUISHED GRADUATE

The United States Naval Academy at Annapolis, Maryland, is a training ground for leaders. Over the years one president, four governors, and many congressmen have graduated from the institution. On June 4, 1996, Jimmy Carter, one of the

* * * *

Academy's most famous graduates, spoke to members of his old class. "When I was five years old . . . if anyone asked me what I wanted to do when I grew up I didn't say I wanted to be a cowboy or a fireman. I said, like a parrot, that I wanted to go to Annapolis. It was a lifetime ambition of mine."

In 1943, when he was nineteen years old, Carter fulfilled his ambition and entered the U.S. Naval Academy. At the time, World War II raged, and Navy ships were engaged in fierce battles on far-flung oceans. Upon graduation most of the young men studying with Carter at the Academy would become officers on those fighting ships. The prospect of being hurled into combat immediately after completing their schooling weighed heavily on the minds of the young students.

Jimmy Carter graduated from the Naval Academy in 1946. He and members of his class were fortunate because by 1946, World War II (1939–1945) had ended. About 15 percent of Naval Academy men who graduated during the war years were killed in the conflict.

After graduation Carter served as a naval officer for seven years. At one point he joined a select crew aboard a nuclear submarine. Carter was forced to leave the Navy in 1953 when his father died. He returned to the small town of Plains, Georgia, where he grew up. There he ran the family farm. He also entered a new profession: **politics**. In 1970 he was elected governor of Georgia. Six years later, in 1976, the American people chose him to be their

U.S. MILITARY ACADEMIES

The Naval Academy at Annapolis is one of four military academies **funded** by the U.S. government. The academies offer college courses designed to train future officers in the United States armed forces. The other academies are: the United States Military Academy at West Point, New York; the United States Air Force Academy at Colorado Springs, Colorado; and the United States Coast Guard Academy at New London, Connecticut.

39th president. Carter credited his success to the training he received at the Academy. As President Carter said when he addressed his former classmates: "I think all of us began to shape or solidify our lives' priorities when we were here."

Carter, who served as president of the United States from 1977 to 1981, is one of the Academy's most famous graduates. He is shown here addressing a town meeting in Oklahoma in 1979.

The waterfront town of Annapolis is the state capital of Maryland.

ANNAPOLIS, THE TOWN BY THE SEA

Naturally, a school that teaches future naval officers must be close to the sea. Annapolis sits on the Chesapeake Bay, which opens into the Atlantic Ocean. The earliest settlers of Annapolis were sternly religious farmers, called Puritans, who established a village there in 1649. The village by the sea later became the capital city of the colony of Maryland.

In 1968, the Maryland State House was designated a National Historic Landmark, meaning that it is significant to our country's history.

HISTORIC STATE HOUSE

In the center of Annapolis rises the red-brick State House (above), where the Maryland **legislature** (called the General Assembly) meets. Begun in 1772, the State House is the nation's oldest state capitol building still in day-to-day use. Over the years many historic events have taken place in the Maryland State House. The United States Continental Congress met there from 1783 to 1784, making tiny Annapolis the nation's capital city during that period. And on January 14, 1784, the Treaty of Paris was **ratified** in the Maryland State House, ending the Revolutionary War.

It was named Annapolis to honor Princess Anne, who later became queen of England. In the colonial years Annapolis hosted a lively theater and opera scene, as well as some lower forms of entertainment; George Washington visited there in 1771 and complained that he lost money at the town's horse races. After the American Revolution (1775–1783), Annapolis was named the capital of Maryland.

Today Annapolis is a charming small city of about 36,000 people. In the city's historic district stand rows of eighteenth-century brick buildings, most of which have been painstakingly restored. Visitors stroll Annapolis's narrow tree-lined streets, which radiate out from the State House grounds. A short walk from the State House is the Annapolis Harbor, which opens into the Chesapeake Bay. Years ago the harbor was crowded with merchant ships and fishing vessels. Now hundreds of yachts and other pleasure boats bob at anchor. Along the harbor sprawls the city's most famous institution—the United States Naval Academy. The school and the city have had friendly relations for more than 150 years.

The beautiful scenery and historic buildings of Annapolis attract many visitors.

⭐ ⭐ ⭐ ⭐

THE ACADEMY IS BORN

The United States Navy was established by the Continental Congress in 1775. At the time, the country was fighting for its independence, and there was little thought about creating a special school to train naval officers. But the need for such a school soon became evident. In 1842, the captain of the naval ship *Somers* ordered three men hanged for the crime of mutiny, an act of rebellion during which crew members try to take over a ship. One of those put to death was Philip Spencer, the son of the U.S. secretary of war. The mutiny shocked the nation and prompted the government to start training professional naval officers who could properly lead crews.

In 1845 George Bancroft became secretary of the Navy. Bancroft was a scholar, a historian, and a schoolmaster. He had long believed the nation should establish a naval school, but he thought that Congress would refuse to provide money for such a project. So Bancroft took $28,272 that Congress had already given the Navy for the purposes of "instruction" and used the money to begin the Naval Academy. Bancroft chose the seaport town of Annapolis largely

George Bancroft established the Naval Academy in 1845. Bancroft was also a notable historian and author.

This illustration shows a view of the Naval Academy in the 1850s.

because it was home to an old Army post called Fort Severn. The new naval school could simply move onto the grounds of the old fort. On October 10, 1845, what is now the U.S. Naval Academy at Annapolis began holding classes. The school's first class was made up of about fifty young students (who were called midshipmen) and seven teachers.

From the beginning the school was run by an officer called the superintendent. The first superintendent was a thirty-year Navy **veteran** named Franklin Buchanan. He was a stocky, broad-shouldered figure. Fellow officers claimed Buchanan was the strongest man in the Navy. He

WHAT'S IN A WORD?

The term *midshipman* was used hundreds of years ago by the British to describe an officer in training whose battle station was amidship, or in the middle of the ship. Today about 15 percent of the Naval Academy's students are women, but they are still called midshipmen. Often the word is shortened, and the students are referred to as *mids*.

11

Franklin Buchanan served as the first superintendent of the U.S. Naval Academy.

once prevented a mutiny simply by standing on the deck of his ship and staring angrily at the rebellious crew members, daring them to lay a hand or a sword on him. No sailor dared get close to Buchanan, and tempers cooled among the seamen. Buchanan House, now the superintendent's residence at the Academy, is named after the school's first leader.

CHANGING WITH THE TIMES

The American Civil War (1861–1865) divided the Academy as it did the nation. Of the 246 midshipmen at the Academy when war broke out, 174 chose to serve with Union (Northern) forces, and 72 joined the Confederates (Southern forces). Union leaders feared the Confederate army would capture and occupy the Naval Academy, so Union officials moved the school to Newport, Rhode Island. It remained there for four years.

This photograph shows the Naval Academy at its temporary home in Newport, Rhode Island, during the Civil War.

13

Neither side could claim victory in the battle of the _Monitor_ and _Merrimack_, but the battle was important because it changed the way ships were built in the United States.

THE _MONITOR_ AND THE _MERRIMACK_

In March 1862, the Union warship _Monitor_ battled the Confederate ship _Merrimack_ (officially the CSS _Virginia_) at Hampton Roads, Virginia. It was a **revolutionary** encounter. Prior to this battle warships were wooden and driven by sails. In this case both ships, known as ironclads, were steam-powered and clad, or covered, with iron armor. This first battle between ironclads changed naval history. In one day wooden sailing ships became useless in war. The _Merrimack_'s skipper was Franklin Buchanan, the founding superintendent of the Naval Academy. The _Monitor_ was commanded by John L. Worden, who became superintendent in 1869.

A new superintendent, David Dixon Porter, took over the academy in 1865. Porter made sports such as baseball, rugby, gymnastics, and rowing a major part of the midshipmen's lives. He also invited the young ladies of Annapolis to campus for parties that included grand dances. Many old sailors criticized these changes, calling the school "Porter's Dancing Academy."

In 1872 the academy admitted James Conyers, its first black midshipman. At the time, many people in the nation had a negative attitude toward

African Americans. Slavery had ended only seven years before, with the close of the Civil War. As part of an **initiation** ritual white students made Conyers sit on a tree trunk and bark like a dog. Conyers dropped out of the Academy after two years of mistreatment. Two other black midshipmen also left before graduation during the early 1870s. More than seventy years would pass before an African American completed a four-year course and graduated from the Naval Academy.

Beginning in 1882 Naval Academy graduates were allowed to become officers in the Marine Corps. The Marine Corps, an **amphibious** invasion force, depends on the Navy to deliver its members to overseas shores. Often the Marines

Members of the Naval Academy baseball team posed for this picture in the 1860s.

Major General John A. Lejeune served in the Marines for more than 40 years.

The Marine Corps, the smallest of all the U.S. Armed Forces, works closely with the Navy.

are called "soldiers of the sea," and they have always worked closely with the Navy. Midshipman John A. Lejeune graduated in the class of 1888 and chose to become an officer with the Marines. Major General Lejeune served as the commandant of the Marine Corps from 1920 to 1929. Lejeune Hall, the Naval Academy's largest gymnasium building, now honors the 13th Marine commandant. Over the years millions of men and women have trained at Camp Lejeune, the huge Marine base in North Carolina. Today up to one-sixth of Academy graduates choose to serve in the Marines.

The Navy's first operational submarine, the *Holland*, was just 53 feet (16 meters) long and held only six crew members.

In the early twentieth century, Academy men pioneered the Navy's efforts in **aviation**. The Navy's first airfield was built in 1911 in Annapolis. Operating from that field, Lieutenant John Rodgers rumbled into the sky in a craft that featured two wings, two motors, and pusher propellers. Rodgers dazzled the townspeople by flying his airplane in a series of spins and loops. Naval planes later roared off the fleet's aircraft carriers.

The Academy also made great strides in the development of submarines—sea vessels designed to operate underwater. One of the Navy's earliest submarines, the *Holland*, was based at the Academy from 1900 to 1905. It was a tiny craft

18

that smelled of gasoline fumes. Sailors called it a "pigboat." Still, many midshipmen volunteered to man this **primitive** submarine and experience the thrill of sailing underseas.

During World War II the United States Navy operated the largest fleet ever assembled in world history. Officers commanding that fleet were recruited from every walk of life. Only about five in every one hundred World War II naval officers were Academy graduates. Yet Academy men distinguished themselves in combat. One was Lieutenant Richard McCool, a junior officer on a landing craft off the Pacific island of Okinawa. On June 11, 1945, two Japanese suicide planes crashed into McCool's ship, engulfing the deck with

The U.S. Navy played a key role in World War II.

flames. Though he was severely burned McCool led crew members below deck to pull wounded men out of the wreckage. He was later awarded the Congressional Medal of Honor, the nation's highest award for bravery.

THE MODERN NAVAL ACADEMY

The Academy righted a historical wrong when Wesley A. Brown graduated in 1949. Brown was the first African-American midshipman to complete the four-year course. As a pioneer, Brown was under enormous pressure to succeed in his studies. Despite the tensions, Brown graduated in the top half of his class. Brown later wrote, "All through my years at the Naval Academy my instructors treated me impartially. I never received special attention, either positive or negative. It was a lesson in democracy which many institutions could imitate."

The post-World War II Navy saw the development of nuclear-powered ships. Such ships use the power of the atom. Driven by nuclear reactors, submarines could stay below the surface for months, and enormous aircraft carriers could circle the globe many times without refueling.

Hyman Rickover, who graduated from the Naval Academy in 1922, is often called the Father of the Nuclear Navy.

In 1949, Wesley Brown became the first African-American to graduate from the Naval Academy.

This photograph shows the USS *Nautilus* entering New York Harbor in 1956.

Born in Poland, Rickover immigrated to the United States with his family when he was four years old. After growing up in poverty, Rickover entered the Academy and got high marks in engineering subjects. Under his direction the United States launched the *Nautilus*, the world's first nuclear-powered submarine, in 1954. Today, Rickover Hall is the Academy's main engineering building.

Another Naval Academy graduate helped the nation soar into outer space. On May 5, 1961, as millions watched on

Alan Shepard is shown here in the *Project Mercury* spacecraft in 1961. He attended the Naval Academy hoping to become an aviator.

television, astronaut Alan Shepard rocketed off the ground from Cape Canaveral, Florida. Just fifteen minutes later his space capsule parachuted to Earth over the Atlantic Ocean. It was America's first manned space flight, and it made Shepard an instant national hero. Alan Shepard graduated from the Naval Academy in 1944 and went on to become one of the Navy's top pilots. Ten years after that historic first flight, Shepard commanded *Apollo 14*, the third spacecraft to land on the moon.

In 1976 eighty-one women became members of the incoming class. Previously it was believed women were unsuited to serve on ships, and therefore females did not attend the Naval Academy. Attitudes change, however, and Naval Academy policies usually adjust to the changes. Today women mids are everywhere on the grounds. Female sailors and officers now serve on most ships in the U.S. Navy.

In more than two hundred years the Navy has graduated from wooden to steel ships and from sail to nuclear power. The Naval Academy has been on the cutting edge of this change. The school is now a major center for engineering and science. And it remains a place where leaders learn.

The Naval Academy offers both men and women an equal chance at success.

Only the best and brightest graduate from the Naval Academy.

JOINING THE ACADEMY

Any American citizen who is at least seventeen and not older than twenty-two years of age can ask for admission into the Naval Academy. But only the best and the brightest candidates are accepted. Every year more than 12,000 young men and women apply to the Naval Academy, but only some 1,200 are admitted. Most students at Annapolis ranked in the top 10 percent of their high school class.

★ ★ ★ ★

The incoming classes reflect America's diversity. Students come from all fifty states. About 15 percent of new students are women, and roughly 20 to 25 percent belong to ethnic minorities.

Why do young men and women want to come to Annapolis? The Naval Academy is, in the words of a teacher, "one of the premier colleges in the world." Courses are taught by some of the nation's finest professors. The education one receives, plus room and meals, is entirely free. In fact, midshipmen are paid. In the year 2003 the average midshipman received a salary of $764 a month from the U.S. Navy. This pay is given for duties as a junior naval officer.

A naval officer poses near a warship in Hawaii.

* * * *

Despite the pay, few midshipmen look upon the Academy as if it were a job. Instead it is the beginning of a new life. Upon graduation midshipmen are expected to serve five years as officers in the U.S. Navy or the Marine Corps. Many Academy graduates decide to make the Navy or the Marines a career, and they stay in the service for twenty or thirty years.

MIDSHIPMAN LIFE

After a person is accepted, the demanding first year begins. Make no mistake, when you enter the Naval Academy you join the Navy. Military discipline rules your life. You are expected to stand at rigid attention when an upperclassman—a student in his or her second, third, or fourth year at the Academy—asks you questions, and you'd better know all the answers. Some of the questions are meaningless and designed simply to challenge the newcomer's power to memorize facts. For example: How many windowpanes are in the skylight of Memorial Hall? Answer: 489. And don't forget to say "sir" when you answer.

An incoming freshman is not called a midshipman; that title must be earned. Instead the freshman is a *plebe*. The word comes from Latin and means "common person." Newcomers are sometimes treated as if they are stupid and know nothing. Therefore some Academy students claim the word *plebe* should be translated as "the lowest form of human life." Whatever its meaning, a student remains a plebe for his or her first year. Plebes are not allowed to own any luxuries, such as personal radios or stereos. A plebe

Many of the training activities during plebe summer test the plebes' ability to work with others and endure physical challenges.

receives his or her introduction to the Academy during "plebe summer," which begins weeks before regular classes start. During plebe summer the freshmen march and exercise under the hot Annapolis sun. Many first-year students compare plebe summer to the tough training program associated with Marine Corps boot camp.

The miseries of plebe year end in May, just before the summer break. But before one graduates from plebe to midshipman a final initiation **ritual** is required. At a given signal plebes rush from Bancroft Hall to a monument called the Herndon. The monument honors Commander

27

William Herndon, who went down with his ship in a storm
in 1857. The Herndon is 21 feet (6 m) tall and shaped like
an **obelisk**.

* * * *

When the plebes gather before the Herndon all gaze at a small sailor's cap that has been placed at its peak. It is the job of the one thousand or more plebes to swarm the monument, remove the sailor's cap, and replace it with a proper midshipman's hat. It sounds simple enough, but upperclassmen have covered the Herndon with 200 pounds of slippery lard. Nevertheless the plebes attack the monument while the school watches and laughs at their efforts. Records are kept. The 1969 class of plebes replaced the hat in a record time of 1 minute, 30 seconds (but that year the monument wasn't greased). The 1995 class took 4 hours, 15 minutes to accomplish the task because that year upperclassmen stuck the cap on the monument with Crazy Glue.

Studies at the Academy are tough. Typical classes include electrical engineering, mechanical engineering, **thermodynamics**, and strengths of materials. All these

A professor supervises a laboratory experiment in class. These students are studying the effect of liquid over various shapes.

technical subjects require strong skills in mathematics. Mids also take courses in English literature, foreign languages, and political science. The Academy offers students more than five hundred classes. Nineteen major subjects lead a student to a bachelor of science degree. As is true with most colleges, midshipmen receive grades of A, B, C, D, and F (for failure). Scoring a B average is difficult at the Naval Academy.

Each class loses about 22 percent of its members before graduation. Some students get discouraged about getting poor grades and drop out. Others are asked to leave for disciplinary or academic reasons. Leaving school before graduation is a sad experience for students, but teachers point out that the Academy's dropout rate is low compared with those of other universities.

Because the Naval Academy is one of the top schools in the nation, its students put in more study hours than at other schools.

* * * *

At the Ring Dance, third year students wear their class rings for the first time to symbolize their commitment to the Navy.

BEWARE BILGER'S GATE

The Bilger's Gate entrance to the Naval Academy is rarely used by midshipmen. In the old days, students who were dismissed or who dropped out of the Academy were required to leave the grounds through Bilger's Gate. Today, students are **superstitious** about the gate—avoid it, they say, or you may end up being "Bilged out."

Midshipmen are allowed periods of fun during the course of their studies. The Academy sponsors a drama club that puts on plays. Men's and women's glee clubs give frequent performances. The annual Ring Dance is a time-honored event. During the Ring Dance, third-year students are allowed to put on their class rings. To celebrate this privilege they lead their dates through a gigantic class ring. They also dip the rings in a barrel of water taken from the seven seas.

On graduation day senior midshipmen stand at attention while a band plays "Blue and Gold," the school's official

31

The hat toss, done for the first time in 1912, is now a traditional ending to the graduation ceremony.

song. Speeches are given and diplomas awarded. Finally the graduates are asked to give three cheers to those they are leaving behind: "Hip, hip, hooray! Hip, hip, hooray!" At the last "hooray" the graduates take off their caps and fling them in the air. This hat-tossing tradition is a great burst of pride for the young men and women. They have paid for their diplomas with hard work and perhaps a few tears. Now they are graduates from one of the nation's finest colleges,

★ ★ ★ ★

and they are about to become officers in the United States Navy or the Marine Corps.

SPORTS AT THE ACADEMY

Four years of physical education are required of all midshipmen. Classes in swimming and sailing are important for future Navy officers. Swimming classes are held at the Olympic-size pool in Lejeune Hall. One diving platform at the pool is 33 feet (10 m) tall and represents the height of an average ship above the ocean surface. All mids are required to jump off this platform prior to graduation.

Other required gym classes include judo, boxing, and wrestling. Beyond regular gym classes the students join

All midshipmen are required to participate in sail training to learn seamanship skills. Many midshipmen also join sailing teams to participate in competitions and other events.

"ANCHORS AWEIGH"

"Anchors Aweigh," the song of the U.S. Navy, was composed at the Academy in 1906. Midshipman Alfred Hart Miles wrote the words, and the Academy's bandmaster, Lieutenant Charles Zimmerman, composed the music. The song describes the ending of Academy days and the beginnings of a career at sea:

Anchors aweigh, my boys,

Anchors aweigh,

Farewell to college joys

We sail at break of day.

SHAPE UP!

All midshipmen must pass a physical **endurance** test that includes the following minimum performances: Men—forty-five push-ups in two minutes and sixty-five sit-ups in two minutes. Women—twenty push-ups in two minutes and sixty-five sit-ups in two minutes. All students must complete a 1.5-mile (2.4-kilometer) run. Men must run the course in ten minutes, thirty seconds; women in twelve minutes, forty seconds.

These cadets are determined to finish their morning jog despite heavy rain and strong winds.

intramural or "club" teams. Favorite club sports are volleyball, soccer, and softball. You will see young men and women jogging everywhere on the grounds. Dedicated workout warriors jog even in the rain and sleet.

The Academy is well known for its football team. Years ago the annual Army-Navy Game (a contest between the Naval Academy and its Army counterpart at West Point) was the nation's most popular football clash. Today the best college players turn professional after they leave school. West Point and Annapolis students, however, are expected to serve as officers after graduation, and therefore the schools do

not attract players who hope to play professionally. Still, stars have emerged at Annapolis. Joe Bellino, a bruising running back, won the Heisman Trophy as the nation's outstanding football player in 1960. Another Heisman winner, Roger Staubach, served as an officer and then became a legendary quarterback for the Dallas Cowboys.

A famous Academy sportsman is David Robinson. Robinson was not an outstanding high school basketball player. He went to the Academy because he wanted a good education and hoped to have a career as a naval officer. On the basketball floor, however, the 7-foot, 1-inch center suddenly sparkled and led the mids to victory after victory. Soon Robinson faced a difficult decision: Should he drop out of the Academy in his third year and collect

David Robinson, a graduate of the Naval Academy, was named one of the National Basketball Association's all-time greatest basketball players.

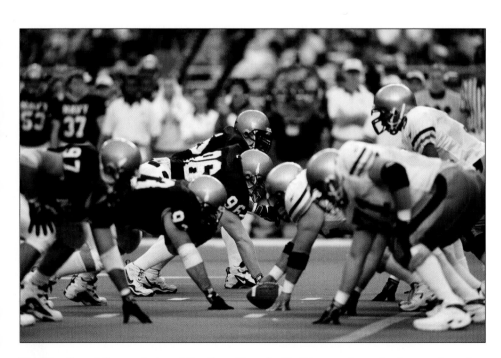

The friendly yet fierce rivalry of the Army-Navy football teams draws huge crowds and loyal fans.

A goat has served as the official school mascot since 1904.

the millions of dollars awaiting him if he signed with a professional team? Robinson decided to stay in school. "I don't live for money," he said. He graduated in 1987 and served his time as a Navy officer. After Robinson's discharge he became an all-pro player for the San Antonio Spurs. Because of his Navy background, sports writers nicknamed him the Admiral.

TOURING THE ACADEMY

The Naval Academy campus is called the Yard, as in shipyard. Every year 1.5 million people from all over the world come to see the Yard. Tourists walk in the shade of hundred-year-old elm and chestnut trees. They marvel at impressive old buildings. They also come to see the midshipmen at work. Admission to the Yard is free. Walking tours, given by knowledgeable volunteers, cost a small fee. School groups are always welcome.

There are so many architectural gems in the Yard that the whole area is designated a National Historical Landmark. This means there can be no major changes to the buildings. Memorial Hall, which is part of Bancroft Hall, is dedicated to Academy men and women who have been killed in wars. Inside Memorial Hall are two elegant crystal chandeliers, a massive skylight, and dozens of paintings of naval scenes. Not far away is Buchanan House, which was completed in 1906. It is the superintendent's residence. Visitors marvel at Buchanan's splendidly kept formal gardens. Towering over all of these buildings is the dome of

The historic Chapel is located in the center of the Yard. It serves as a reminder of the importance of religion in our country's history.

the Academy Chapel. The Chapel, whose construction dates back to 1904, is sometimes called the Cathedral of the Navy. Shaped like a Latin cross, the Chapel seats 2,500 worshipers.

Bancroft Hall, named after the one-time secretary of the Navy George Bancroft, is often called the world's largest college dorm. Bancroft covers about 32 acres (13 hectares)

The remains of John Paul Jones lay in Bancroft Hall for nearly thirteen years before he was moved to his final resting place in the Chapel in 1913. Midshipmen at the academy carry on his legacy and are inspired by Jones' brilliant naval career.

THE FATHER OF THE U.S. NAVY

Within the Chapel is the grave of John Paul Jones. Born in Scotland, John Paul Jones (1747–1792) fought for the American side in the Revolutionary War. During one sea battle a British officer demanded he surrender his ship, and Jones replied, "I have not yet begun to fight." Today many historians call Jones the Father of the U.S. Navy. He died in Paris, where his grave remained for 113 years. In 1905 his remains were moved to the United States and placed—fittingly—in a permanent crypt, or underground chamber, at the Naval Academy.

and has five floors, 1,873 rooms, and 5 miles (8 km) of hallways. The mids live in this huge building, two to four students per room. Most learn to love the old place, and they call it Mother B. The hall was opened in 1904 and has had many additions since then.

Three times a day the midshipmen eat together at Bancroft's T-shaped dining room, called King Hall. Feeding four thousand or more hungry young men and women is a daunting task for King Hall's kitchen staff. Here are a few statistics: The kitchen

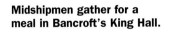

regularly broils 4,000 hamburgers, makes 750 gallons (2,839 liters) of soup, bakes 1,200 loaves of bread, and scoops out an average of 300 gallons (1,136 l) of ice cream each day. On holidays it roasts 320 turkeys. What is the midshipmen's favorite dish? This is a matter of debate, but many insiders claim the students love a fried treat called chicken fingers.

Tecumseh Court spreads opposite the main entrance to Bancroft Hall and thus sits in the center of student life. Dominating the court is a statue of the Shawnee warrior chief Tecumseh. Over the years the statue has become the source of legends. He is the lord of football. Mids paint the statue with gold and blue war paint before each Army-Navy game. He is also the charm figure of good grades.

Midshipmen offer pennies to Tecumseh to bring them luck on their final exams.

★ ★ ★ ★

Students facing a tough exam toss a penny at the statue in hopes that Tecumseh's spirit will grant them a few extra points on the test.

A must for every visitor is a tour of the U.S. Naval Academy Museum. Housed in Preble Hall, collections at the museum are as old as the Academy itself. Swords, pistols, paintings, prints, uniforms, and centuries-old cannons are on display. The museum owns more than six hundred historic American flags, including the one flown at the Battle of Lake Erie (1813), where a dying captain told his mates, "Don't give up the ship." Another American flag at the museum was carried by astronauts on the moon. The pride of the U.S. Naval Academy Museum is the Gallery of Ships, an exhibit of superbly crafted model sailing vessels. Sitting under glass, the models depict sailing ships from 1650 to 1850. It is among the most valuable collection of model ships in the world.

Visiting the Naval Academy is a thrilling experience for tourists. For midshipmen, who stay there four years, the Yard holds a lifetime of memories. The United States Naval Academy is one of the finest colleges in America. Above all it is a place where leaders learn.

* * * *

**FAST FACTS ON THE
U.S. NAVAL ACADEMY**

• The Yard has 195 buildings,
75 monuments, 15 miles
(24 km) of walkways,
13 miles (21 km) of roads,
and 7 fields for sports
or parades.

• The student population is
about 4,200.

• About six hundred teachers
work at the Academy.

• It costs the U.S. government
about $240 million each year
to run the Naval Academy.

A museum employee carefully examines a model ship. Many of these valuable models
are the only record left of these historical ships.

Glossary

amphibious—capable of moving on land and water

aviation—the science of flying aircraft

endurance—the ability to continue doing an activity, sometimes despite pain, for a long period of time

funded—paid for

initiation—a ceremony or event to introduce something or someone

legislature—a congress or other government body that writes laws

obelisk—a four-sided, usually tapering stone used for monuments

placard—a written announcement displayed in a public place

politics—relating to the government

primitive—roughly constructed, crude

ratified—given formal approval, as with a treaty or
other measure

revolutionary—a complete change

ritual—a ceremony or custom

superstitious—relating to a person's strong belief
about something that is not realistic or supported
by facts

thermodynamics—the science of the relationship
between heat and other forms of energy

veteran—a person who has experience serving in
the military

Timeline: Annapolis

1649	1775	1839	1842	1845	1861	1865

1842 — A mutiny on board the ship *Somers* triggers a public demand for the nation to train professional officers for its ships.

1845 — The United States Naval Academy at Annapolis is opened; the school is made up of fifty students and seven teachers.

1861 — Fearing an attack by Confederate forces, the government moves the Naval Academy to Newport, Rhode Island.

1865 — The Civil War ends, and the Academy returns to Annapolis.

1649 — Puritan farmers establish the village of Annapolis in the colony of Maryland.

1775 — The Continental Congress creates the United States Navy.

1839 — The Navy's first steam-powered vessel is built, creating a need for engineers as well as sailors.

1872	1882	1890	1911	1949	1976	1995
			The Navy's first airfield is built at Annapolis.	Midshipman Wesley A. Brown becomes the first African American to graduate.	The Academy admits eighty-one female students.	The Academy celebrates its 150th birthday.

1872	1882	1890
James Conyers becomes the first African-American to be admitted at the Academy; he drops out after two years mainly because of brutal treatment.	Annapolis graduates are allowed to become officers in the United States Marine Corps.	The first Army-Navy football game is played; Annapolis students win 24-0.

To Find Out More

BOOKS

Gaines, Ann Graham. *The Navy in Action*. Springfield, NJ: Enslow Publishers, 2001.

Schraff, Anne E. *Jimmy Carter*. Springfield, NJ: Enslow Publishers, 1998.

Simmons, Clara Ann. *The Story of the U.S. Naval Academy*. Annapolis, MD: Naval Institute Press, 1995.

Tibbitts, Alison. *John Paul Jones: Father of the American Navy* Springfield, NJ: Enslow Publishers, 2002.

ONLINE SITES

United States Naval Academy's Official Site
http://www.usna.edu

U.S. Naval Academy Museum
http://www.usna.edu/Museum

U. S. Navy's Official Website: Welcome Aboard
http://www.navy.mil

Index

Bold numbers indicate illustrations.

American Revolution, 8

Annapolis Harbor, 9

Army-Navy Game, 34, 39

Bancroft, George, 10, **10**, 37

Bellino, Joe, 35

Bilger's Gate, 31

Brown, Wesley A., 20, **20**

Buchanan, Franklin, 11, **12**, 13, 14

Carter, Jimmy, 4–6, **4**, **6**

chapel, 37, **37**

Chesapeake Bay, 7, 9

Civil War, 13, 15

Congressional Medal of Honor, 20

Conyers, James, 14–15

Fort Severn, 11

Gallery of Ships, 40

graduation day, 31–33

Herndon Monument, 27–29, **28**

historic attractions, 8–9

Jones, John Paul, 38

King Hall, 38–39, **39**

Lejeune, John A., **16**, 17

Marine Corps, 15, 17, 26, 27

Maryland State House, 8, **8**

mascot, 36, **36**

McCool, Richard, 19–20

midshipmen life, 26–27

Miles, Alfred Hart, 33

Plebe, 26–29, **27**, **28**

Porter, David Dixon, 14

Preble Hall, 40

Puritans, 7

Rickover, Hyman, 20–21

Ring Dance, 31, **31**

Robinson, David, 35–36, **35**

Rodgers, John, 18

Shepard, Alan, 22, **22**

songs, 31, 33

Spencer, Philip, 10

sports, **15**, 33–35

Staubach, Roger, 35

submarines, 18, 20

Tecumseh, 39–40, **40**

U.S. military academies, 5

U.S. Naval Academy
fast facts, 41
joining, 24–26
origin, 10–13
studies, 29–30
touring, 36–37

USS Nautilus, 21, **21**

Warships, 14, **14**

Washington, George, 8

West Point, New York, 5, 34

women in Naval Academy, 22–25, **23**, **24**

Worden, John L., 14

World War II, 5, 19

Zimmerman, Charles, 33

About the Author

R. Conrad Stein grew up in Chicago. He enlisted in the U.S. Marines at age eighteen and served three years. He later attended the University of Illinois and graduated with a degree in history. Mr. Stein is a full-time author of books for young readers. Over the years he has published more than one hundred books for various publishing companies. The author lives in Chicago with his wife, Deborah Kent (who is also an author of books for young readers), and their daughter, Janna.

To research this book the author made a very enjoyable trip to Annapolis and the Naval Academy. Mr. Stein wishes to thank the guides, the instructors, the midshipmen, and others who treated him so well while he was at the Academy. To all the mids he adds: GO NAVY!